Where are they going?

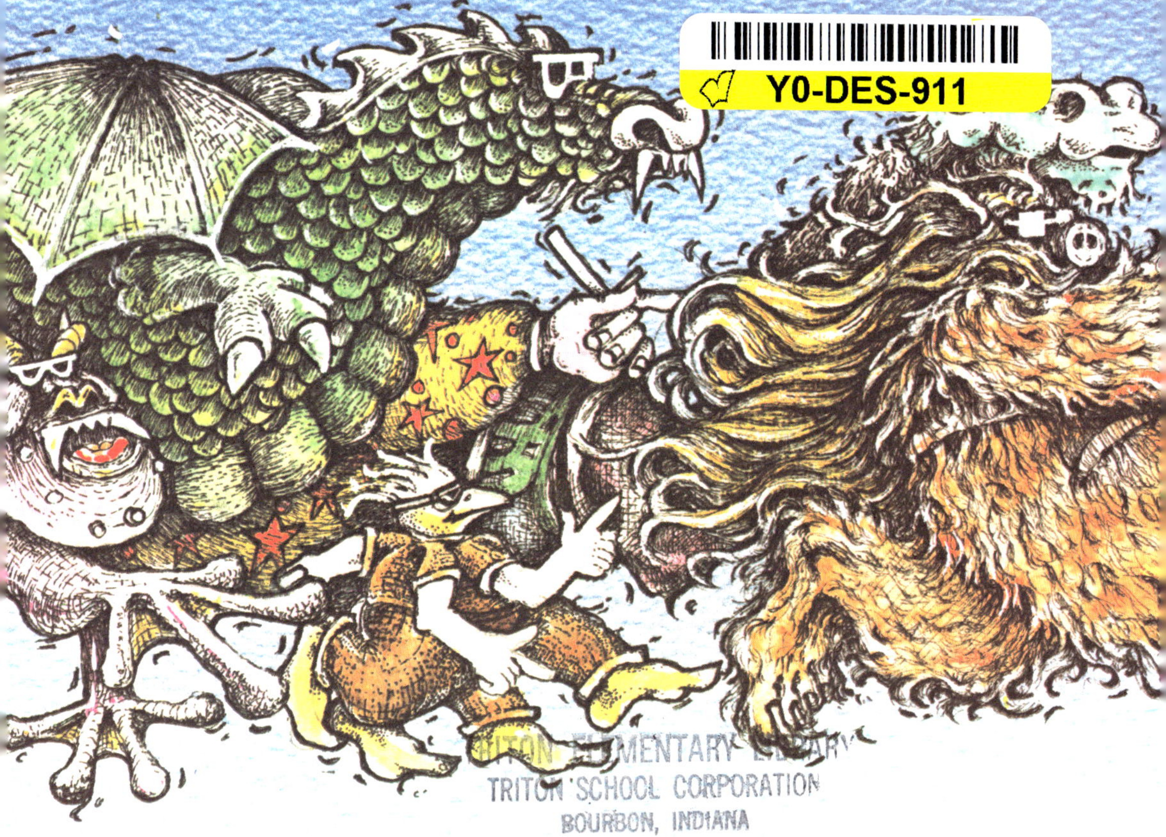

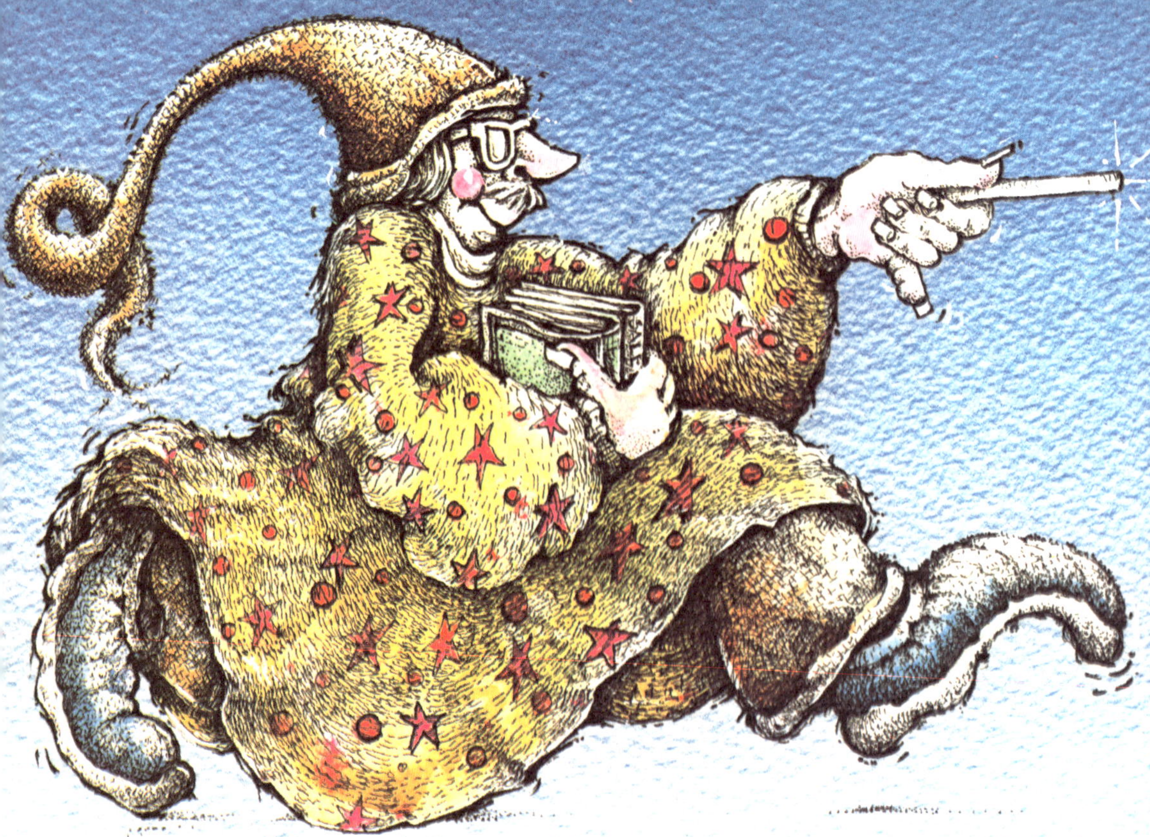

Look! Here is a wizard.

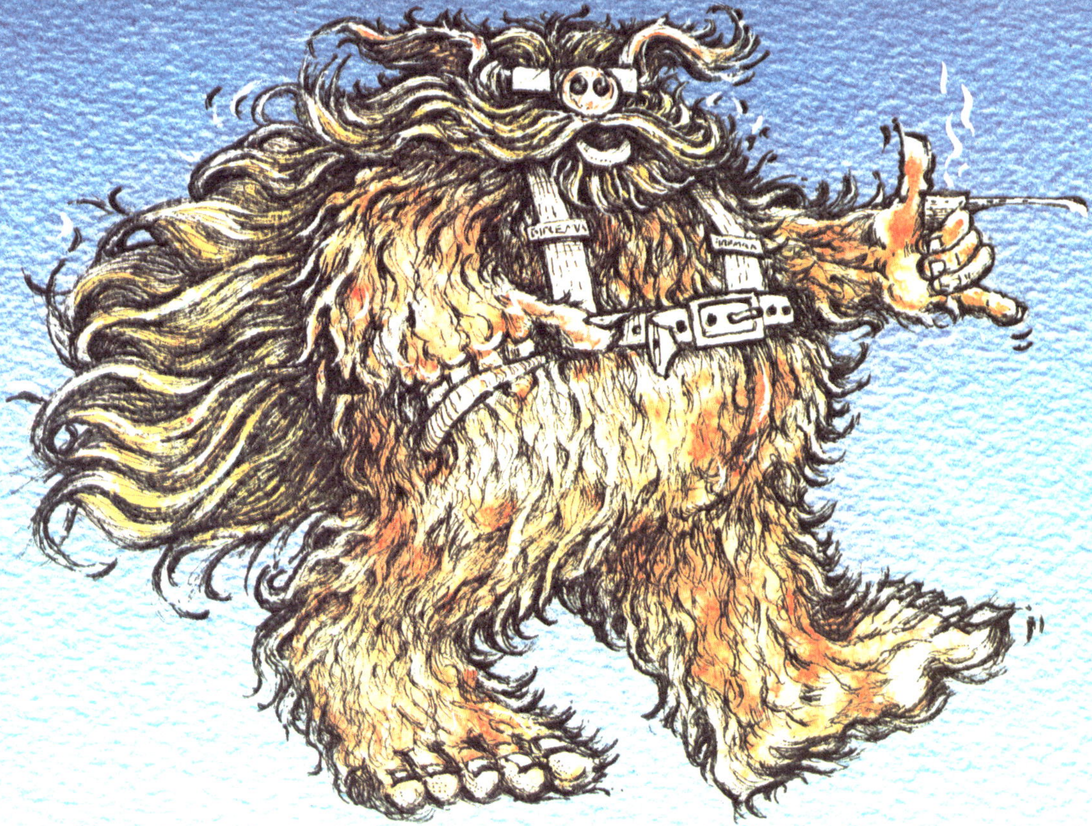

Look! Here is a hairy thing.

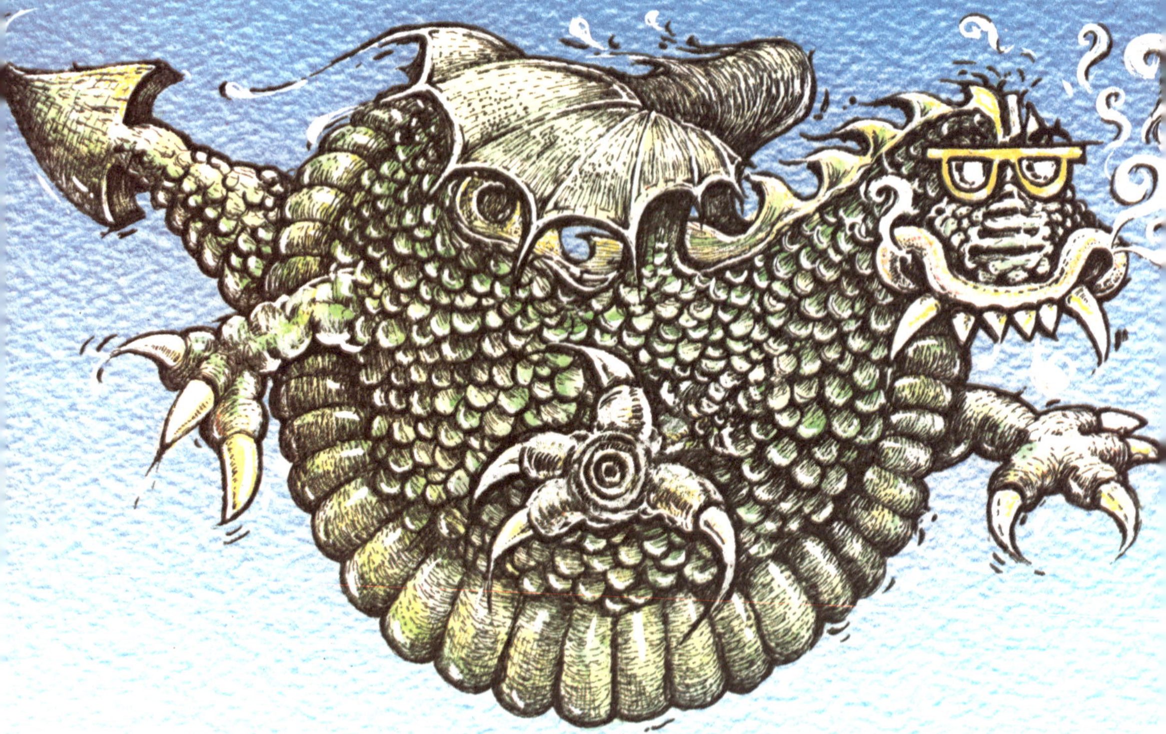

Look! Here is a dragon.

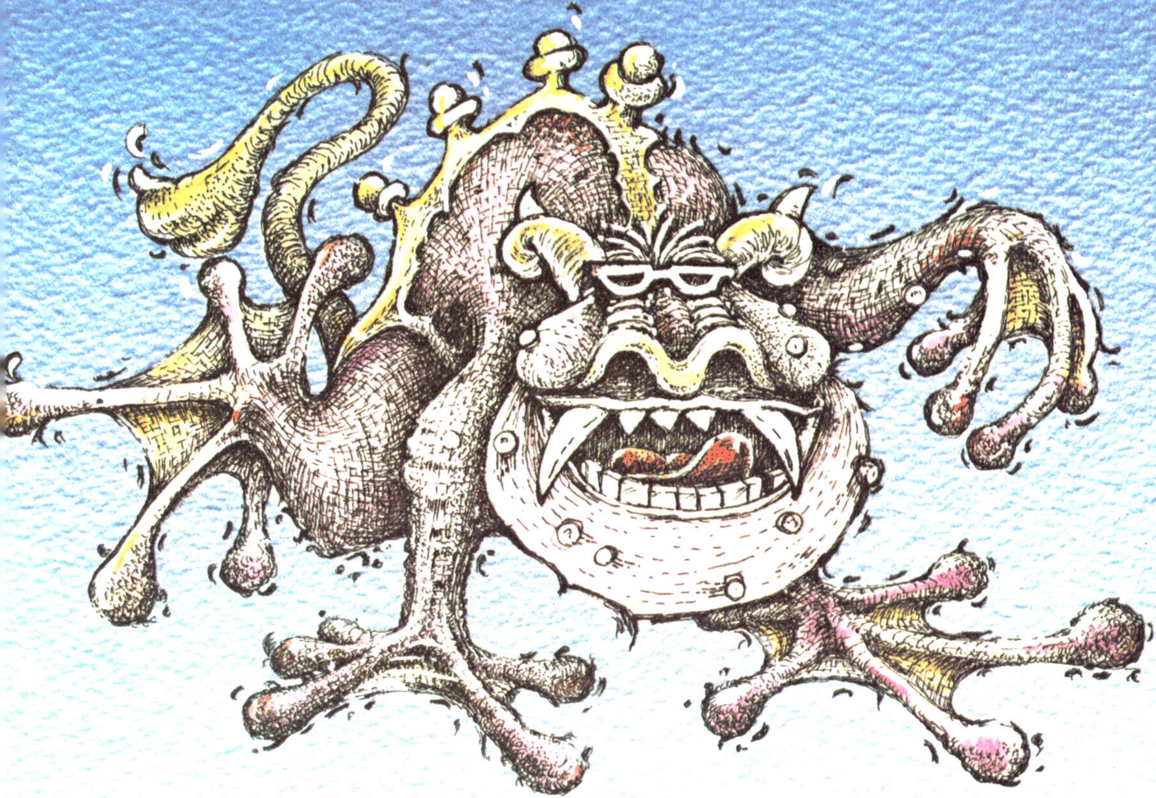

Look! Here is a scary thing.

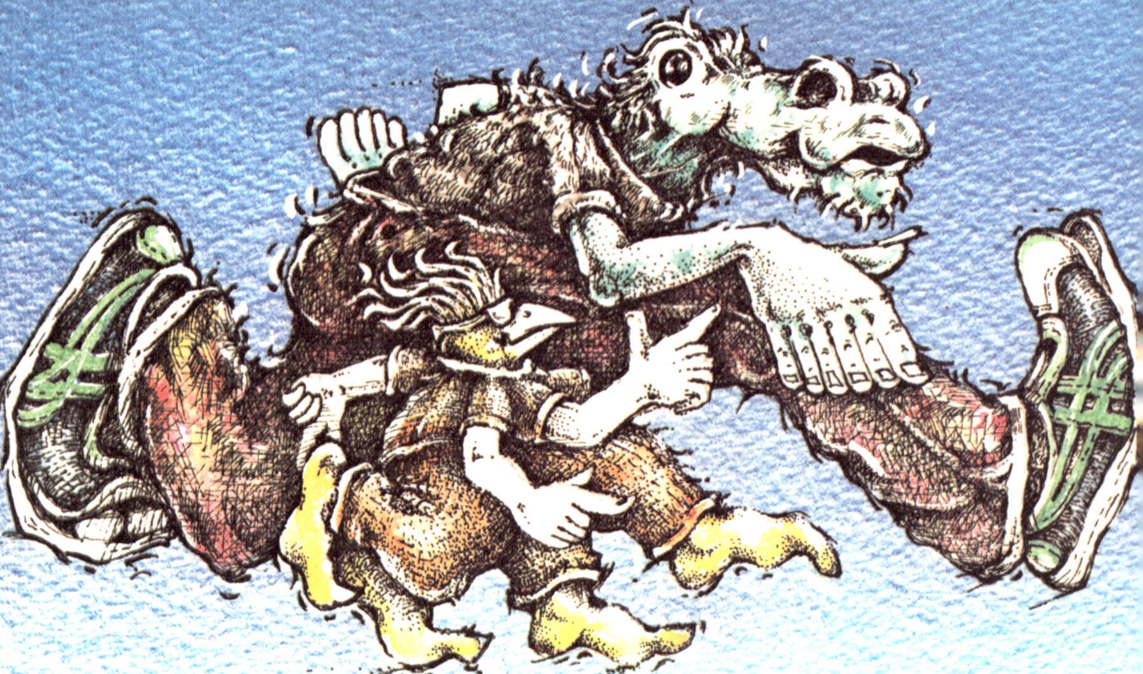

Here is a tall thing,
and here is a small thing.

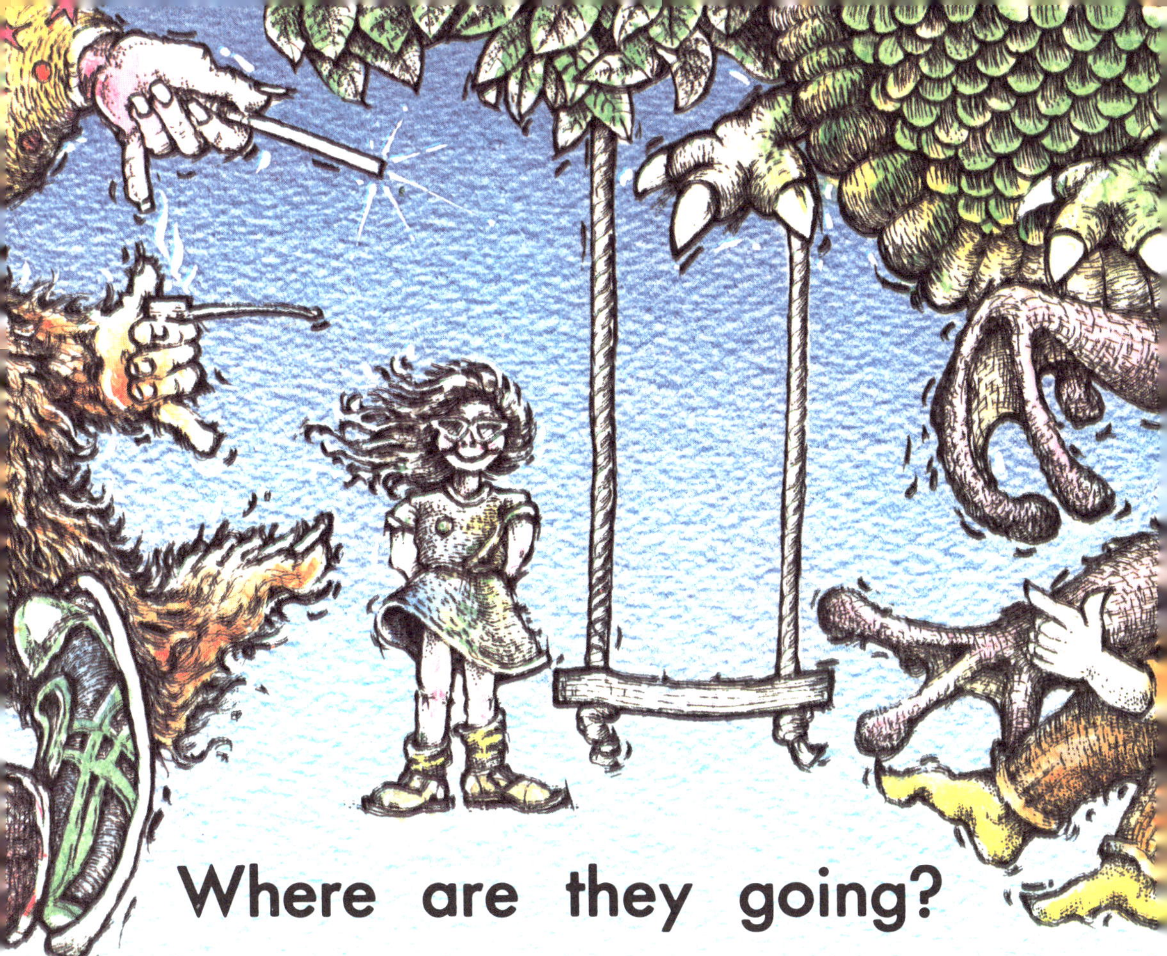

Where are they going?

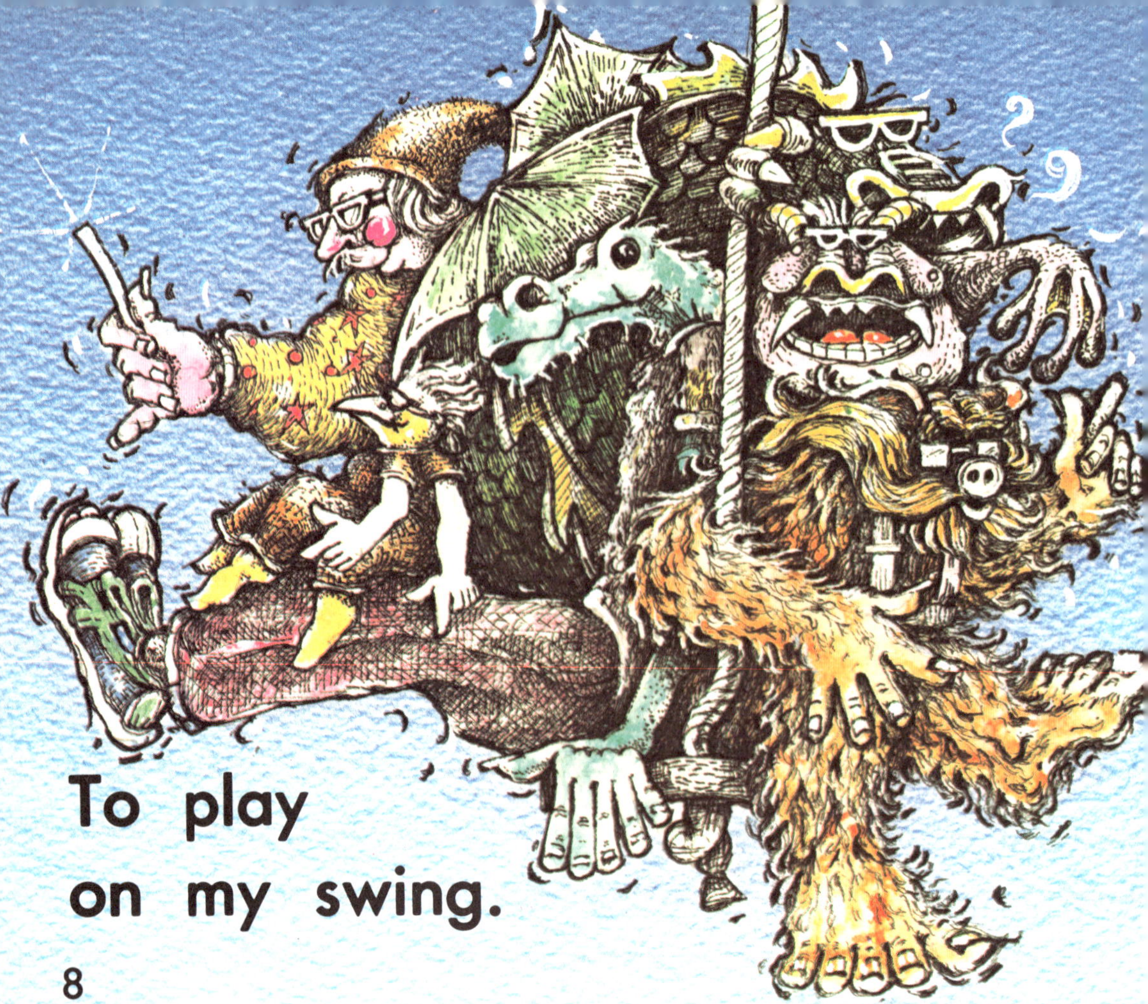

To play
on my swing.